T0131812

My Soul Cries Out

Cries Out

Visitation, Poetry of Love, Repentance, and Forgiveness

Lynita Paschal-Hammonds

AuthorHouse™
1663 Liberty Drive
Bloomington, IN 47403
www.authorhouse.com
Phone: 1 (800) 839-8640

Published by AuthorHouse 01/03/2019

ISBN: 978-1-5462-4022-8 (sc)
ISBN: 978-1-5462-4023-5 (e)

authorHOUSE®

My Soul Cries Out

Visitation, Poetry of Love, Repentance, and Forgiveness

Lynita Paschal-Hammonds

Biography

My name is Lynita Paschai-Hammonds born and raised in Atlanta Ga. I am one of fourteen children with two lovely children of my own. After many years of suffering silently from clinical depression as well as physical, and emotion abuse I can without a doubt testify of The Most High love and mercy in my life. His almighty power and holy presence is evidence to redemption and salvation. And because of this reality I live.

This book of poems and visitations was written to uplift, inspirer and encourage those who are burden and who carry a heavy heart. To share the power of love, forgiveness and hope to the hopeless an a voice to those who suffer silently.

It will reveal some of my own personal wars and triumph. This journey called life is all apart of our heavenly father love for me and you. Although we live in a sinful world age that will impact our lives, relationships and most of all our spiritual connection with our heavenly father. Know that he has promised us that he will never leave nor forsake us.(Hebrew 13:5)

Remember one of the purpose of this earth age is about free will. God our creator has allowed us to make our own hearts and minds up as to whom we will serve. Will we follow the Messiah our savior or Satan the serpent whom is the deceiver and accuser?

It is important that we understand that we each must make up our own mind, as to how we will live life, and also to know that true repentance of sins in the name of Yahusha the Savior is readily available for all.

We each must take personal responsibility for our own character defeats. Through prayer, self-examination and by admitting to God, yourself, and another our wrongdoing. Once these key steps are practice as often as is needed you will then began to live a more happier life.

I will lift up mine eyes unto the hills, from whence cometh my help. **Psalm 121:1**

Special Thanks

First, I would like to give all the praise to my Lord and Savior Yahusha for
his love and mercy, and who is the forgiver of all my sins.

Thanks to my dad (George RIP) and to my mom who is living (Mattye)
for life, love and being my first teachers of Holy Word.

Thanks to Lee Garrett my special friend and for your support.

Thanks to my sister Veronica, thanks for your encouragement throughout the process of the book.

Thanks to my two lovely children Dorian and Tyrah and ex-husband (Orlando)
and also to all of my family and friends for their constant prayers.

I love you and may The Most High be with you all.

Lynita Paschal-Hammonds
nenepaschal@icloud.com
Llph1967@gmail.com

Contents

Clinical Depression

A mood disorder causing a persistent feeling of sadness and loss of interest.

Mental illness is a conversation that needs a bigger platform for discussion.

This is a chemical imbalance in the brain it does not discriminate, regardless if you are rich or poor have beauty or fame anyone can be a victim.

One of the problems I see is a lack of education. "We the People". We must all be more aware of this condition, from the individual to the parents, teachers, ministers, employers as well as family and friends, being that such an illness can have a negative impact on us all.

We are seeing the loss of life or after effects of this illness in our schools, homes, jobs, churches, and communities. Although science is helpful with providing medication, it is not the only answer to ensuring a quality of life.

However, the positive answer is to educate. Early diagnosis, support groups, balanced lifestyle, and public awareness is very important.

This illness, like many others, such as cancer, diabetes, muscular sclerosis, and other disabilities should be out in front. Not only should we talk about it when disaster strikes but from the humanity standpoint.

So let us begin to help with a daily healing of the disease though love and education

By: Lynita Hammonds

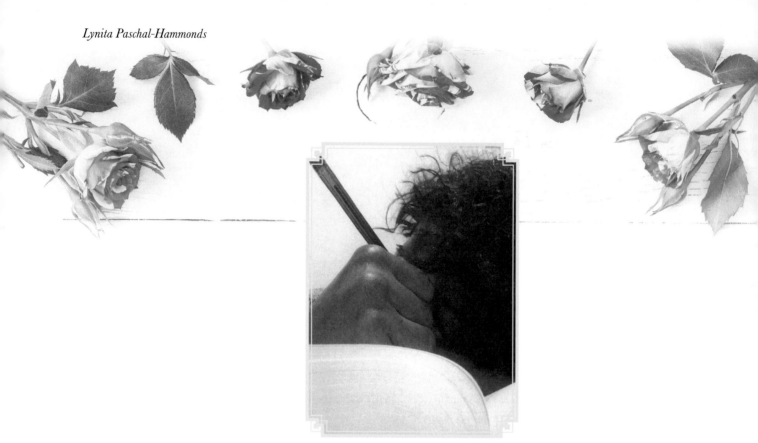

This story is written for children who deal with severe depression or mental illness. It is to show how young children who may have severe illness, and are not educated or aware of this illness may suffer silently. Neither do he/she know how to explain the pain or the daily struggles of how to cope and live each day.

Mommy I don't feel like going to school today.

I have already been up most of the night, and it feels like I've been in a fight Tossing and turning, body aching, mind racing, cuz I ain't hardly got no sleep. I'm not going to learn my lesson with all the kids teasing and messing with me.

I don't understand it anyway, no, not at all! I just don't understand me, so please could everyone leave me be so I can get some sleep.

1st visitation

I was laying in my bed, when suddenly the power of the Holy Spirit came upon me, and showed me this. I was praying in the basement at my church, when I looked around and saw what appeared to be an angel. He was dressed in a long white robe, and his hand was stretched out toward me. He said,"come". I began walking toward him and we joined hands. I was holding his hand tight as we walked together.

Quickly we arrived at a strange looking place that looked like a big underground cave. We walked through the door using no handles, and when we had gotten inside it was very dark and gloomy.

Oh my God! There were people there and they were screaming and crying in such loud voices and the turmoil on their faces was horrifying. As we continue walking through, the Angel said to me." look and see"! And so I did. There were many! Many there and I began to cry.

I felt sadness and fear! And it was then, when the Angel looked at me and said to me "be not afraid". One of the tortured spirits reached out for me, and I pulled back. I could see them crying but couldn't help. So I said to the Angel with tears rolling down my face," please get me out of here". And so he did!

As we were leaving, we began walking on a straight and narrow road and the road was steep. When we reached the top of the hill, one stopped. In front of us was this beautiful castle, and there were two guards on each side of the door. And I said to the Angel," please can I go in there? But he turned around and looked at me with a smile and a bright glow and said "blessed is he who endure to the end".

I immediately fell on my knees and faced down and began praising Him. When

I looked up he was gone!

Lp 1982

Adolescent years

We can all remember something about our teen years. Good or bad, these are impressionable life changing moment. One thing for sure, it is when we are beginning to learn who we are, and what we like or dislike about ourselves and others.

This is a special time that shape our views about life, culture, and spirituality, and has some of the greatest impact in our lives.

With love, education and hard work is when we believe our dreams can come true. It also give us a solid foundation and identity in which we can stand upon during some of the most challenging times such as pure pressure.

At this time, I am 14 teen years of age, but what this young lady does not know is that how her life will change now and in five years. I was just beginning to form my own relationship with The Most High. And have experience my first visitation.

Afterwards will be the poem who also a critical violation that would take me many years to heal

WHO

Who is going to tell her that winter is near

Who

To dress in layers of clothing my love because your travel may be long

Oh and here is some food for your hunger, water for your thirst, and the good book for companionship

Who

Who is going to tell her, take your compass for direction and your rod and shield for protection

Who

Who is going to tell her many tears she will   shed, dangerous predators lay ahead, and an enemy who wants her dead

Who

Who is going to warn her, that the   pain inside her   heart would run deep like the ocean, mountains to climb that are tall and steep, so look straight ahead my love, straight ahead

Now don't be afraid but endure and stay strong, because you my love is never along.

Lph 02/2017

 *Lynita Paschal-Hammonds*

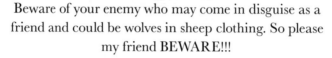

Beware

Beware of your enemy who may come in disguise as a friend and could be wolves in sheep clothing. So please my friend BEWARE!!!

This segment is about rape. And following are the three poems that from such a violation to any human being can leave the victims state of mind and spirit lost.

It is very hard to transition back to life as the norm. However through the love and mercy of our Lord and Savior Yahusha who is the healer of all pain can help us to overcome.

Remember forgive us our trust passes as we forgive those who trust passes against us.

Matthew chapter 6:5

Lph 97 /98

RAPE

You robed me of my dream and fantasy
You even tried to rob me of my destiny

You made me cry without knowing why
At time I thought to myself I might even die

You held me captive and had your merry way
The shame! The guilt! The pain and my innocent you took

And my voice was silenced on that day, not a scream, nor shout,
only fear and doubt that laid deep within my spirit.

But hold on juts a minuet, you didn't win it, you see
Because of The Almighty God, I have been set free.

Llp 07/2007

Anger

Women in the mirror, who are you?

My days or dark, mind in rage cause I
am sick and tired of being sick and quiet

Like oil hitting the firer my
temperature rise higher every time I
think about you.
See, I am angry right now and don't
want to confined

So out come my emotion from the up
And downs of life roller coaster, which
sometimes catches you off guard.

LPH 1997

Spiritual Confusion

Woman in the mirror, who are you?
I am experiencing delusions have you know conclusion.

How many are there is the question you have for me
There are many you see, enough to keep your mind from reality.

I am not just a figmet of your imagination; I am as real as can be
I am spiritual confusion

LPH 1997

Loneliness

Women in the mirror! Your tears are falling constantly.
Like a waterfall ceaseless.
Isolation is the feeling inside the way darkness is in the dessert.
Emotions escalating and descending and you are losing all control.
Thanking you heard a voice when actually it was just a thought
Reaching out for someone, but feel there is no comforter.
Frustrated and depressed from the consuming pain, but no one to blame.
Think you're going insane? No dear.
Loneliness is my name.

Lph 1997

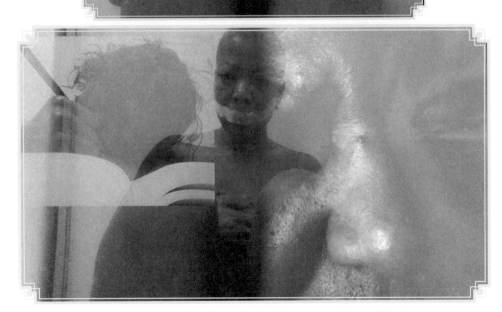

In this picture is three photos in one representing the lost of identity
By: Lynita Hammonds

By Lynita Hammonds

Until We Meet Again

Into my womb, you arrived
I was only able to feel your presence for a little while

We felt each other's love
So soft and sweet
Soul to soul
Heartbeat to heartbeat

Before I could hold you, it was time for you to go
Back to The Heavenly Father leaving me to hope

So now, is the time for me to be strong
Someday we will meet again when I return home

Lph 01/2016

Forgive Me My Sweet Child

My sweet sweet love
Into my womb you came from heaven above
I never did give you w chance to love
Not to speak, play or to teach

Forgive me for denyiny you of your dreams
To be married, to have children, and to be seen

Nor did I think of your human rights
I just let you go without a fight

I am not the creator of life and by my own selfishness did wrong by you, instead of what was right

I am asking you my sweet love to please forgive me my sin

Lph 2016

A Soul in Need

You sneak around like a snake in the night, doing the things of evil.

And in the morning you put on your fancy attire and speed off to work, looking the part of dignified person.

Your soul is thirsty
Belly is empty
And your mind is filled from the worries of the day

Need a ride but everyone keep passing you by
Looking in your wallet for cash and all you find is trash

Yelling at the kids because there is no help for already full hands
No food on the table
No friendly ear to listen

Bring it to The Most High! Casting all your cares upon him, because he cares for you.

1 Peter 5:7

Lph 06/2017

Facing the enemy (visitation and dream)

I had a dream that I was in bible study class. There was others in class with me as well. The teacher of the class name was Holy Filled. And in this class mine eye was open. We was giving home work and class was then dismissed.

I was then awaken by the sound of rain tapping on my window. And as I laid there with my eyes closed all of a sudden, I could see this spirit hovering over me. This spirit was ugly and felt unclean. It was as if it was trying to smoother or kill me.

I began to fight back. And it went away. I sat up quickly and began to look around the room, and saw that know one was there, and that my family was still asleep. My heart was beating fast and i thought to myself "what was that". So I laid back down and slowly drifted back to sleep.

I began to dream. And in my dream I see myself and many other women in this room. It was two of us to one bed. One at the top and one at the bottom. The room was dark and everyone appeared to be asleep. But I was not. There was a light in the hall way. And it was than I saw what appeared to be a man coming in the room where all of us was. He had a very evil or dark appearance. He walked over to me. He leaned his face down to me to see if I was asleep and I said unto him "I see you".

He than straighten up turned around and walked away. As he was leaving I can hear The Holy Spirit say unto me " get up, you are going to have to fight". And so I jumped up out of the bed and went for it.

The dark and evil spirit turned around to face me and we began to fight. Me and the dark spirit was fighting in the hallway going back and forth. I fought it with all of my strength and my might like my life depended on it.

There was steps in the hallway, and I pushed it down the stairs. I could see him laying flat on his back near the bottom of the steps. I sat at the top of the stairs weeping and crying. I was tired from the battle and thought he was dead.

And as I am looking at him, suddenly two very bright lights with angelic appearance dressed in long white robes came in through the wall or a side entrance. And they said unto me "he is not dead you must cut off the head". So I said unto them with fear upon me I cant. And they said unto me, come we will help you.

So I went to them and the body of the dark and evil spirit was now laying on a table. And together they gave me a knife they helped me cut off the enemies head. The two angels than went out the same entrance that they came in, and I followed them as well. It was then I saw me standing on top of mountains. Many many mountains! With faces that are like angelic lions, beautiful and indescribable they were. And I was dancing and shouting praises to Yahua.

Lph\1998

Your debt

And I had this dream these two that was parent was standing before a table, that had many, many bills laid on it. And as they both stood behind the table, and a few of us children was there. Suddenly I heard the mother speak and she said, " I cant pay all these bills, but the father never said a word. There was fear and sadness upon her face. And then three of the children picked up a bill from the table, each to pay one of the bills and I awaken from the dream.

Lph /1998

Open doors

I had a dream that I was walking through doors. And every time that I would walk through one door I would have to walk through another door. And another door. And this went on and on, door after door. I remember that know door was the same. Straight ahead, around the corner, up and down the way it went. Door after door it was. I became so exalted.

So much to the point to where I thought about giving up or that, I was not going to make it. Finally, I came to last door and by now, I am literally crawling on my needs. So when I open the final door, I had come to a room. The room was the size of guess bedroom. And the room had no furniture or people there, just a window. And the window was open.

So as I am on my needs so completely drain from all the walking through the doors, but in my spirit, I am so thankful to have made it. This is when I hear a voice like a soft wind say unto me "come and look out the window". And so I did. And when I had did I was so amazed because I was so high up in the ski that I was looking down at the stars. It was breath taking. Magnificent being so high up in the heaven and witnessing how Great Our Heavenly Father is.

This is when I hear The Heavenly Father speak and say unto me "I Am GOD". I immediately fell to the floor and I said, "Yes Lord I know". And the dream ended.

Lph 2013

Lynita Paschal-Hammonds

not my father?

I had a dream that I was in the house that was not my own and some of my family was
there also. And there was this man who looked like my birth father, and he was in a
chair with his hands tied behind him and he was pleading door some coffee.
And as each of my family members that would try and make him coffee, he would kick them back.
And he said to them that he wanted me to do it, and that I was the only one that could.
And so I tried, so as I went to the coffee pot to make the coffee he wanted me to make for him the blender
went out of control and the coffee was spilling all over the place, but about less than half stayed in the cup.
And as I passed to the man who appeared to be my father, and fed him what little I could, he drink it.
Again I was not in my home, and was unable to give him a full cup. And then I awaken from my sleep.
I was so disturb by the dream, and I thought to myself, why was my dad hands tied? And
I wonder why was he wanting only me to make him coffee? And why coffee?

Lph 05/2016

Guess who is coming to town

He is saying bring me your sick and shut in
Want a physical or spiritual healing
Need prosperity
Having problems with your love ones
Got love on your mind
Need a friend, a savior
Want some medical or cosmetic surgery
Are you hungry
Got drugs, and drinking problems
Want to tell me your heart desirer
Want wings to fly
What about peace and no more wars and hatred
How about a word for today
Come! Come and follow me and we will all just……. love! love! love!
Stop! Wait a minute. Not in this life time in this earth age. If you happen to run
across this man that spinning lies with all his guys, rebuke that demon in the name
of Yahusha and tell him to go back to hell from whence he come.
Warning! Please read. (Matthew 24 and Mark 13)

I am pregnant

I had a dream that I was pregnant. I went to the doctor for a physical and the doctor said unto me" you are pregnant with child" let me deliver your child. I said unto him no! Not now! I left his office and went to another doctor who said unto me" you are pregnant with twins".

He said one has a heartbeat, but the other does not. Let's get you ready to for delivery. I said unto this doctor, "not now, I am waiting for the father.

In this dream the fathers name was milo. And then I awaken and looked up the name milo which might be from the old Slavonic root milu (merciful) or milos which in Slavonic means pleasant.

Lph 04/2017

11/2017

Deceiver

You told me that you love me, as if I was blind and couldn't see.

Willing and dealing with my emotion all the time lying too me.

Like a cheap casino or game of spades, you place your bet.

Laughing out loud drawing a crowed and waiting to cast your net.

Setting the rules and thinking you was smooth all the while my clock was ticking.

Trying my patience with no consideration. Lack of respect and no regret.

OHHH! I see you.

What kind of thing are you? That you would convince yourself to believe your own lies.

Haven't you read the quote "you reap what you sow". If only you knew, that lies will catch up with you, and that's the truth.

One day, you will come to know. That playing your silly games is just ashame with no one to blame but you.

Lph 06/2017

Yahuah gave me power over the enemy

So I had this dream that I was in my parents home. And many of there children was there. I was down stairs in the kitchen cooking salmon. And I only had one can which was not enough for the size of my family. Anyway as I cooked the patties and the more family that would come to eat , the more salmon patties would show up on the plate.

I had fed my mom and she said that she was still hungry and had not eaten. So again I fixed her another plate and gave it to her myself. Inotice that my dad who was in the dream didn't speak a word. And as I continue to cook, I was so amazed by what was happening with only one can of salmon.

So after everyone had eaten It was time for me to eat myself, and as I got ready to eat another one of my brothers showed up. I only had my plate, but couldn't let him go without, so I shared my meal with him by dividing my meal with him.

And as I began to feed myself my portion it failed. I than heard all the commotion going on up stairs, and though I'll go see what was happening. And everyone was in my parents room being entertain by my brother or one whom appeared to be my brother.

Oh he had them all laughing. Oh, yes indeed! He was putting on a show for all of them. So I looked at him closely and I saw that he was naked! I mean you could see his front private part all the way to his back side. And he got into my parents bed and was playing and moving in it.

And as he got out of there bed and stood up, I said unto them" yall that's a snake". And I turn around to leave, but before I could complete my turn I saw out the corner of my eye him coming for me. This is when I turned to face him and I grabbed him by the neck and through him down to the ground.

I than place my feet on his neck, and thought to myself if he move I would kill him. So there he laid with his neck on the end of the top steps and his body laying down the rest. And I was awaken

Lph 06/2017

Lynita Paschal-Hammonds

A letter to my sisters

Sisters it's time to wake up now! You have been asleep too long. Can you
hear the voices of our men and children crying out for you?
They are saying that something is wrong with my beautiful flower. Where is she? The one
who use to stand tall and strong. Her beauty was as a rainbow of many colors.
She had a fragrance you could smell a mile away. It was like walking
through a garden of roses on a sunny spring day.
She would hold her head up high because she was proud to be women. A special one whom Yahua
created to be a help meat to mankind. One whom he made perfect to multiply his creation.
She carried herself with dignity because it was a part of her feminity. However, I am sad to say
that my flower, my beautiful one has fallen asleep. What must we do to awaken her?
My heart is broken and shattered like a glass, in many little pieces. Sisters! Oh my beautiful
one. Can you hear me calling you? Let not my tears and my prayers be in vain.

Lph 97/98

A letter to my brothers

BROTHER BROTHERS! I once saw you as a king with a ring that gave me your stamp approval.

Protection and strong and a place to belong was just a few of your basic quality

Love and wisdom you shared

You were not afraid to tell me you cared

Nights under the moonlight we walk hand to hand

And please was I to let the world know you was mines

Our heart was as one and your priority came before fun

A days work! A days Pay! Brother you was earning your way

Long hours and sometimes no shower you was handling things

You were proud of your role, because you had visions, dreams and long term goals

Looking to the heavens for answers because you believe in he that created you

And blessed was your family and community too

Why my brother is the question I ask?

You have left me in charge so you can bend over and show your ass for a little cash?

Lynita Paschal-Hammonds

You have left our home, long gone, and in places you don't belong

Now your women is stripping

Children is sipping

And your world is slipping

Cause the road you traveling is not the way

Stand up straight

Dust yourself off

Because the game your playing is going to cost

So come! And let our hearts commune

Knowing time is short and Our Savior will return soon

Lph 06/201

Yahuah set me free

I am in this place

Gave up my space back in Atlanta G. A.

See I was whining and dining.

Drinking and lying all the while dying a slow death.

Confused and abuse.

Pains and sorrows, and no hope for tomorrow. I think I'll have me another drink.

Until one day from a disaster along came the master of life.

Tapping me on my shoulder and said unto me

I am the way, truth and the life. John 14:6

Then came heart palpitations

Truth and inspirations

Feeling so real

I was broadcasting thrills

Love is real

Lynita Paschal-Hammonds

And I do want to live

Happy and free

Moment by moment

Day by day

Because Yahusha is the way.

Lph 07/2017

LOVE is Yahuah

LOVE...you are my reality, my vision and my dream

LOVE...you are the reason why I sing

LOVE...you are my refuge, my hope each day LOVE...how excellent is your name

LOVE...Excellent and radiant is your beauty above all beauties

LOVE...you never fell nor sleep

LOVE...how marvelous is your council to me

LOVE...you are sweet like honey, comforting and strong LOVE...thank you for correcting me even when I am wrong LOVE...you are amazing magnificent and wise

LOVE...you never left my side

AND

LOVE...how blessed am I to be created by you, to feel your glorious presence, experience your mighty power is the reason why I praise you.

Lph 2017

Believe

You got to willing to live or die for what you believe.

The sun so bright

Moonlight by night

And stars that cover the ski when you believe.

Some even cry when you believe

Cry! And hold your head up high

Not for foolish pride you see.

We are all tested like metal in the firer

When you believe

Spoken or unspoken words revealing it truth

Vision and dreams and those who scheme

Pains and sorrows and no hope for tomorrow will shape you

Or break you according to what you believe

Experiencing highs and lows

Filling lost and uncertain

All the while praying your change gone come

If you believe

Well! If believing is that strong, why not believe in LOVE!

Lph 2016

Printed in the United States
By Bookmasters